HOME PLANNERS'

50¢
60¢ in Canada

92 LOW COST *Ranch* HOMES
FROM $8000 to $18000

by

RICHARD B. POLLMAN
DESIGNER

PALMQUIST & WRIGHT
ARCHITECTS

16 SCALE MODEL HOUSES IN FULL COLOR
SPECIAL SECTION OF 1½ STORY HOUSES

CONSTRUCTION BLUEPRINTS
AND MATERIAL LISTS ARE
AVAILABLE AT LOW COST
· SEE BACK PAGE ·

ANOTHER OUTSTANDING
BOOK OF DESIGNS—

by
RICHARD B. POLLMAN

featuring
100 HOME DESIGNS

BLUEPRINTS FOR BUILDING AVAILABLE AT LOW COST

PLUS

17 PAGES OF FIREPLACE IDEAS **FOR YOUR NEXT HOME**

HOME PLANNERS, *Presents*

92
LOW COST
Ranch
HOMES

by

RICHARD B. POLLMAN
DESIGNER
PALMQUIST & WRIGHT
ARCHITECTS

FROM

$8000 to $18000

CONTENTS

ALBERT P. WITTMAN   publisher

CHARLES W. TALCOTT   editor

Convenient Living

BOOK #12

HOME PLANNERS, INC.
16310 GRAND RIVER • DETROIT 27, MICHIGAN

Published by Home Planners, Inc. for Beacon Publishing Corp., 211 East 37th Street, N.Y.C. Copyright by Home Planners, Inc. 1955. Printed in U.S.A.

FOREWORD

Today, home building in the United States is reaching a new high

level of activity. As a result, we as Americans are becoming known

as a nation of home owners. As the country's building activity

continues to grow, so does the prospect of furnishing not only adequate

but well conceived homes for Mr. and Mrs. America. In view of recent

legislation which has resulted in more liberal home financing terms

through the Federal Housing Authority (F.H.A.), the prospect for

more homes for more Americans becomes more of a reality.

The designs in this book fall, for the most part, within the $8,000 to

$18,000 building budget. Some of the larger homes shown may still fall

into this category by adhering to moderate but good building specifications.

Doing some of the work himself would give the owner added assurance

that his home would stay within the $18,000 price range. It is to those

people in search of a well designed home to fit their limited building budget, that

this collection of home designs by Richard B. Pollman is dedicated.

INDEX TO DESIGNS

3

HOMES UNDER 1000 SQ. FT.

Your next home, however small, does not have to look like a match box. Nor does it have to satisfy only the barest of family requirements. Proper designing can produce a delightfully appealing exterior which surrounds a practical, economically built floor plan with a maximum of convenient living features. Study the designs in this section with an eye to their exterior appeal, the practicability of their floor plans and the economy of their simple rectangular construction.

DESIGN K 263
912 SQ. FT., 16,416 CU. FT.

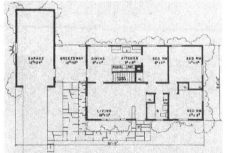

This economical-to-build and clean-looking design provides a full basement, an efficient in-line kitchen, and an all-purpose breezeway for years of proud home ownership.

DESIGN K 314
971 SQ. FT., 9,311 CU. FT.

Here is a lot of home for those desiring compact and efficient room arrangement. The entrance centralizes traffic and allows movement in any direction. The bedroom area is completely isolated to assure privacy. The extensive well positioned closets insulate against sound. Stone planting area in front and covered porch off the dining room are but two of the many aides to convenient living in this home.

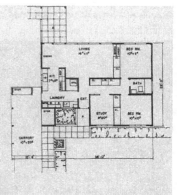

The available blueprints for this home include details for building all four of the exteriors shown here. A good example of how quarried stone can enhance the appearance is shown in the elevation at the top of the page. All exteriors have at least a stone planter.

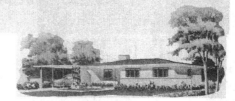

DESIGN K 138
960 SQ. FT., 9,360 CU. FT.

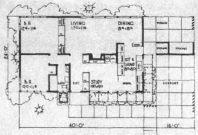

The generous glass areas will provide the proud owner of this home with a view in any direction. Note the abundance of closets, built-ins and storage space.

DESIGN K 232
732 SQ. FT., 8,784 CU. FT.

A small home does not mean your days of having dinner guests are over. This enticing home provides maximum utility. Notice how the overhang eliminates that "match box" appearance.

DESIGN K 147
802 SQ. FT., 14,400 CU. FT.

Here again is plenty of storage space, a most efficient kitchen with a large nook, and a spacious living room tailored for attractive furniture placement. The china closet provides an interesting back drop for the dining area.

DESIGN K 139
960 SQ. FT., 9,360 CU. FT.

Who wouldn't go for the interesting arrangement of this design. Its rectangular shape makes it economical to build, too. The alternate basement plan is included with the blueprints you order.

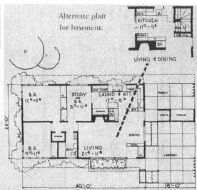

Alternate plan for basement.

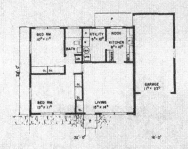

DESIGN K 81
832 SQ. FT., 9,65) CU. FT.

This design shows how any or all sash in a panel type window can be made to swing open. Did you see how little space is used for the hallway?

DESIGN K 149
906 SQ. FT., 16,700 CU. FT.

Note the convenient traffic circulation, the abundant storage areas, and that third room which can, in both plans, serve your needs as a study, an activities room or an extra bedroom.

DESIGN K 231

982 SQ. FT., 10,802 CU. FT.

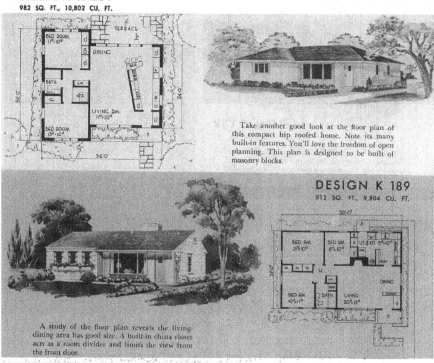

Take another good look at the floor plan of this compact hip roofed home. Note its many built-in features. You'll love the freedom of open planning. This plan is designed to be built of masonry blocks.

DESIGN K 189

912 SQ. FT., 9,804 CU. FT.

A study of the floor plan reveals the living-dining area has good size. A built-in china closet acts as a room divider and limits the view from the front door.

DESIGN K 222

912 SQ. FT., 16,872 CU. FT.

Here's evidence that an economical-to-build rectangular shaped home does not have to look like a box. The trellis work and the planting boxes, together with the expansive living room windows, create freshness of character.

DESIGN K 272
960 SQ. FT., 10,080 CU. FT.

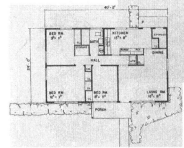

Here is the acme in low cost homes—including a family size kitchen, a plentiful supply of closets and storage space, a step-saving layout, economical one stack plumbing, and a contemporary design that eliminates unnecessary waste of materials.

DESIGN K 257
926 SQ. FT., 12,038 CU. FT.

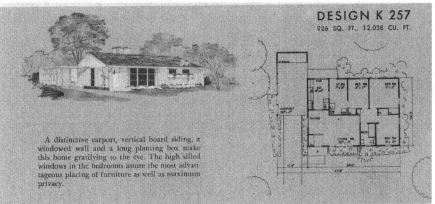

A distinctive carport, vertical board siding, a windowed wall and a long planting box make this home gratifying to the eye. The high silled windows in the bedrooms assure the most advantageous placing of furniture as well as maximum privacy.

DESIGN K 307
912 SQ. FT., 9,800 CU. FT.

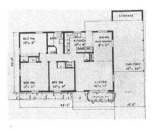

Here is an example of open planning to achieve space. Semi-permanent partitions close off the living-dining areas when desired. Note the compact kitchen-laundry and the location of the heating unit. The carport has storage units of its own.

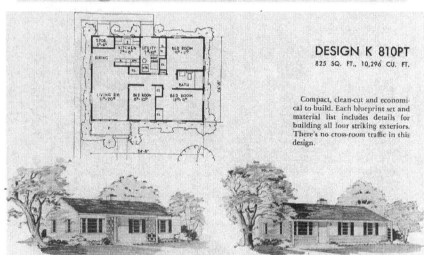

DESIGN K 810PT

825 SQ. FT., 10,296 CU. FT.

Compact, clean-cut and economical to build. Each blueprint set and material list includes details for building all four striking exteriors. There's no cross-room traffic in this design.

DESIGN K 820PT
858 SQ. FT., 15,817 CU. FT.

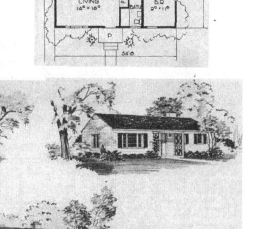

Compact, efficient! . . . Convenient living is ingeniously expressed in this three bedroom design with four different front elevations. Construction costs are at a minimum with a maximum of good living. Here is a house that is engineered to keep material cutting and waste at a minimum.

HOMES 1000 TO 1200 SQ. FT.

The medium sized low cost home with proper designing can be made to appear almost pretentious without being awesome. Careful attention has been given to good proportion, excellent balance and pleasing exterior details. Study the exteriors of this section and you will not find an awkward one among them. The larger floor plans continue to exhibit the same amount of forethought as in the previous section. In many cases there is that extra room, or bath, or additional storage space. Whatever is added, nothing is lost to waste space.

DESIGN K 521
1,178 SQ. FT., 20,310 CU. FT.

This long, low modern ranch home would never fail to impress passersby. The center entry means good traffic circulation. The high windows provide maximum privacy and allow for more flexible furniture placement. The floor-to-ceiling windows of the living room provide a sweeping view of the rear yard. Don't miss the extra washroom and the four storage units in the entry and the hall.

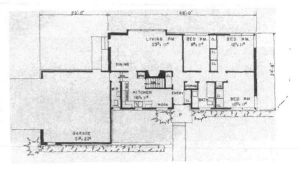

DESIGN K 56
1,037 SQ. FT., 18,362 CU. FT.

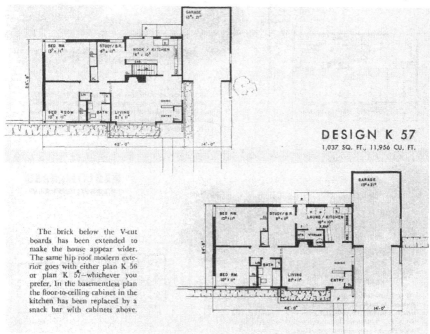

DESIGN K 57
1,037 SQ. FT., 11,956 CU. FT.

The brick below the V-cut boards has been extended to make the house appear wider. The same hip roof modern exterior goes with either plan K 56 or plan K 57—whichever you prefer. In the basementless plan the floor-to-ceiling cabinet in the kitchen has been replaced by a snack bar with cabinets above.

13

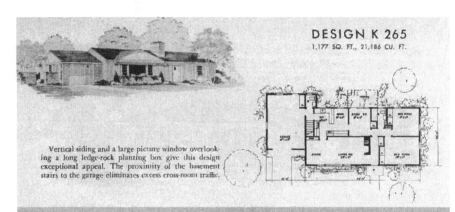

Vertical siding and a large picture window overlooking a long ledge-rock planting box give this design exceptional appeal. The proximity of the basement stairs to the garage eliminates excess cross-room traffic.

DESIGN K 47
1,095 SQ. FT., 10,908 CU. FT.

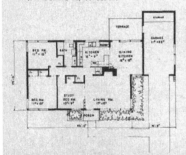

A pleasing combination of a low pitch roof, panel type windows, wide horizontal and V-cut vertical siding, and a brick planting area with an interesting trellis make this home a real charmer. Study the floor plan. Observe the use of folding doors.

DESIGN K 53
1,178 SQ. FT., 20,978 CU. FT.

If you had this up-to-date brick and stone hip roof home on your lot, you'd be enjoying the luxury of a twenty-six foot living-dining area with an eighteen foot panel window. The study and nook could be combined into an all-purpose area.

DESIGN K 51
1,185 SQ. FT., 13,527 CU. FT.

Study the efficiency of layout: center entrance contributing to good traffic circulation; a convenient kitchen with nook; abundant storage facilities; plus an oversize garage. Notice how the stone and V-cut boards provide relief for the brick work.

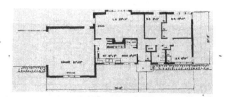

DESIGN K 316
1,124 SQ. FT., 20,980 CU. FT.

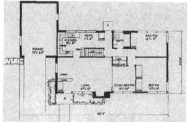

Strong horizontal emphasis and a nice distribution of mass characterize this snug house designed for a small family. Large glass areas light the living-dining area. The study is separated from the living room by a semi-permanent partition.

DESIGN K 285
1,034 SQ. FT., 10,782 CU. FT.

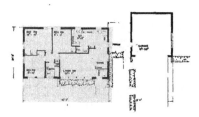

A big "little" house. The covered porch and garage make this house seem larger than it really is. But despite its size, you find three bedrooms and ample space in the living, dining, kitchen and laundry areas.

Alternate plan for basement.

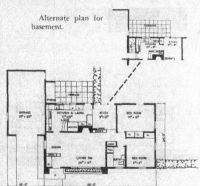

DESIGN K 131
1,008 SQ. FT., 11,340 CU. FT.

Observe the charm of an Early American style home with its exterior of field stone and horizontal siding. The large picture window of the living room overlooks an attractive planting box. Note how the study may be closed off by the use of the draw drapes. List the many other features.

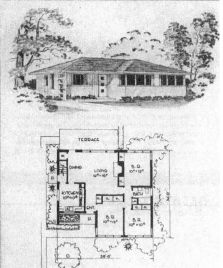

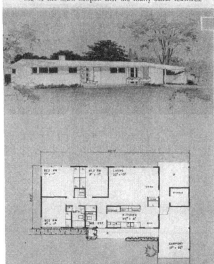

DESIGN K 422
1,152 SQ. FT., 11,174 CU. FT.

This modest sized basementless home provides three fair sized bedrooms and a generously proportioned living-dining area. Ample provision for storage has been made not only in the bedrooms, but in the kitchen and dining area as well.

DESIGN K 142
1,146 SQ. FT., 20,642 CU. FT.

The answer to a homemaker's dream. Imagine, nine closets in this compact house! Study the efficient layout of the kitchen, and don't miss the location of the basement stairs near the grade door. The working plans by Palmquist & Wright, Architects, show details for all wardrobe closets, cabinets and built-ins.

DESIGN K 270
1,197 SQ. FT., 17,848 CU. FT.

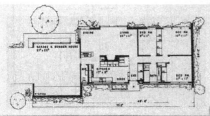

Study this plan carefully. The shoulder high windows on the front make furniture placement easy. The floor-to-ceiling brick fireplace wall, the ceiling slanted with the roof, and the floor-to-ceiling windows give the living-dining area a cheerful warmth.

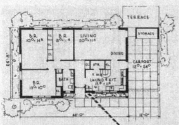

DESIGN K 145
1,062 SQ. FT., 12,744 CU. FT.

Cross room traffic is cut to a minimum without wasing space in this beautiful home constructed of block. Noteworthy is the layout of the work area. Observe the snack bar in the basementless plan, and the nook in the floor plan for the basement.

Alternate basement plan.

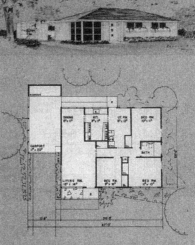

DESIGN K 258
1,008 SQ. FT., 11,876 CU. FT.

In this low-slung hip roof contemporary design you have such big home features as: three bedrooms, ample utility space and good traffic circulation. The big low windows capture the beauty of the planting area.

17

DESIGN K 357
1,144 SQ. FT., 21,564 CU. FT.

Always eye-catching is this complementing combination of horizontal bevel lap boards and vertical V-groove boards neatly set off by quarried stone lower front. The room height thermopane window counterbalances the high sill front bedroom windows, and solidity is enhanced by the smooth, unbroken door surface.

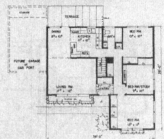

DESIGN K 227
1,177 SQ. FT., 20,106 CU. FT.

This brick veneer home has a vertical board and batten front. The combined fireplace and woodbin near the attractive window will add charm to the hours spent in your living room. Don't miss the built-ins. Blueprints for this design show alternate breezeway and garage details.

DESIGN K 319
1,107 SQ. FT., 19,479 CU. FT.

Best memories of childhood often center around a fragrant country kitchen where warmth and friendliness abounded. The folding wall may be drawn across to hide the kitchen section if desired. If funds must be budgeted, carport and terrace can be added after initial construction is finished.

18

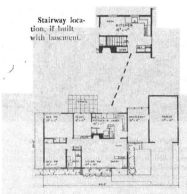

Stairway location, if built with basement.

DESIGN K 133
1,040 SQ. FT., 11,480 CU. FT.

A draw drape in the study, a snack bar in the kitchen, a fireplace in the living room and a china in the dining all contribute to a lifetime of enjoyable living. A basement recreation room version of the plan, prepared by Palmquist & Wright, Architects, is included with each set of blueprints.

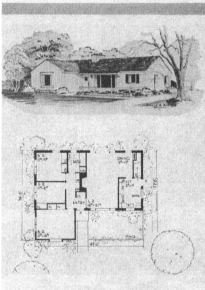

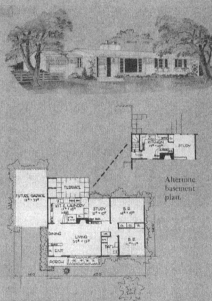

Alternate basement plan.

DESIGN K 183
1,130 SQ. FT., 21,470 CU. FT.

Here is a smart, three bedroom home to go perfectly on that moderately sized lot. A front-to-rear living room with a fireplace, an efficient kitchen with no cross room traffic, and a full basement are noteworthy features.

DESIGN K 128
1,008 SQ. FT., 11,340 CU. FT.

If you like the exterior characteristics of a real ranch home, this design is for you. Study the floor plan. Blueprints by Palmquist & Wright, Architects, show details for construction both with and without basement.

DESIGN K 362
1,128 SQ. FT., 11,337 CU. FT.

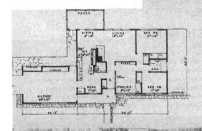

Beauty and practicality, the heart's desire of the ranch style home owner, are soundly applied here. The built-in kitchen arrangements, the combined study and bedroom, the high sill windows which allow leeway in furniture placement, will make the owner's enthusiasm contagious.

DESIGN K 324
1,182 SQ. FT., 11,201 CU. FT.

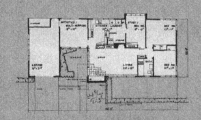

A design with character should have exterior features that distinguish it from the unimaginative home. Harmony is achieved by use of horizontal wood siding, quarried stone and corrugated plastic privacy fences. The activities room and outside terrace provide both indoor and outdoor play areas for the children.

DESIGN K 248
1,012 SQ. FT., 10,322 CU. FT.

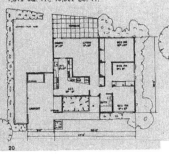

This captivating design combines gracious living with maximum utility. Note the many spacious closets and storage areas. It is unusual to find the kitchen and activities area together in a home of this size.

DESIGN K 360
1,153 SQ. FT., 20,140 CU. FT.

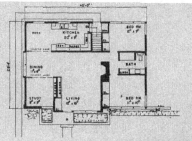

This charming modern with its built-in features will give you the most of the best in convenient living. Notice the folding doors which can be installed to alter the shape and size of three areas. Here is beauty in glass and stone, accentuated by the wide, low roof.

DESIGN K 179
1,132 SQ. FT., 22,086 CU. FT.

The ideal combination of compactness and roominess is embodied in this well balanced alignment of home and garage. The roomy breezeway can easily be converted to add living space. The quarried stone will lend itself beautifully to the landscaping of the grounds.

DESIGN K 249 1,032 SQ. FT., 10,485 CU. FT.

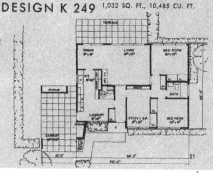

This low slung frame and stone home packs a lot of living for its size. Notice how you can by-pass the study when it's in use; and how the kitchen-laundry leaves plenty of room for eating or baby's play. Large windows overlook the terrace.

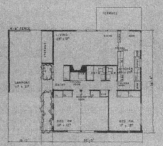

The inside bath, recently sanctioned by the F.H.A., means low plumbing costs when located next to the washroom or kitchen. Observe the relative positions of these areas in this plan. The folding door of the bedroom area greatly increases the utility of a large room.

DESIGN K 274
1,117 SQ. FT., 21,275 CU. FT.

That 40 foot lot remains no problem when it comes to building this design. The hip roof, built-in gutters and panel windows give it that up-to-date look. Notice how the dining area is set apart from the living area without creating a cramped feeling. There's nook space in the kitchen.

DESIGN K 42
1,144 SQ. FT., 13,728 CU. FT.

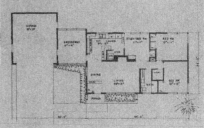

Two fireplaces, built-in china, desk cabinet, snack bar and vanity, and plenty of closets and storage space are the highlights of this plan. The dotted lines represent easily opened and closed folding doors and walls.

DESIGN K 419
1,152 SQ. FT., 11,059 CU. FT.

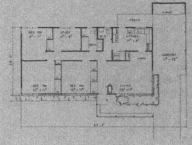

Horizontal lines of the roof overhang and the wood siding emphasize that appealing low slung effect. The extension of the porch roof to the carport assures sheltered access whatever the climate. The convenient location of the washroom in relation to the rear door eliminates through-house traffic.

DESIGN K 367
1,064 SQ. FT., 11,970 CU. FT.

The low hip roof and spacious, flat-roofed carport porch lend width to this smart home. The floor plan gives big room living with moderate sized room efficiency. The U-shaped kitchen affords ample nook and utility space. The fireplace, always in full view, adds to the feeling of size to the living and dining areas.

DESIGN K 181
1,194 SQ. FT., 22,925 CU. FT.

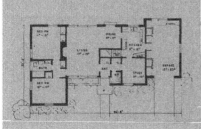

The efficient kitchen is in nice relation to the dining-L and to the study. This room may serve as a guest room. The washroom is handy. There are two closets in the hall. The hobby garage is entered through the kitchen. Notice the six storage units. Observe the central location of the front entrance.

ABOUT THE BLUEPRINTS

The blueprints for the designs appearing in this book have been made available directly from Home Planners, Inc., who also publish home plan books featuring the outstanding work of

1. HOW MANY SETS OF BLUEPRINTS SHOULD BE ORDERED? To study a plan in greater detail than shown in the book, one set will be sufficient. If you are planning to build, then a total of three to six sets may be needed (depending upon circumstances, one each for contractor, owner, building permit, mortgagor, F. H. A., V. A., and tradesmen).

2. WHAT DOES EACH SET OF BLUEPRINTS CONSIST OF? From two to eight large sheets, depending upon the type home involved. Each set shows all dimensions views, details and elevations necessary for a professional builder to complete the home. The location of the electrical outlets and switches, the plumbing fixtures, and the heating plant are also shown. A twelve page specification outline is included with each blueprint order. It lists over 150 phases of construction (from excavating to painting) for you and your builder or architect to agree upon and fill in.

3. HAVE THE PLANS BEEN APPROVED BY F. H. A. AND V. A.? Even though our plans have been drawn to meet or exceed the F. H. A. or V. A. construction requirements, each home owner using F. H. A. or V. A. services must submit his own blueprints for approval by the field office nearest him.

4. WILL THE PLANS MEET LOCAL BUILDING CODES, CUSTOMS AND CONDITIONS? In most cases, yes; because our homes have been engineered for sound construction. However, as long as there are almost as many different codes as there are communities, there are bound to be some cases of conflict. Because these cases are rare, there is no need for concern before securing blueprints for the plan of your choice.

5. CAN MATERIAL SUBSTITUTIONS AND MINOR CHANGES IN LAYOUT AND DESIGN BE MADE? Yes, oftentimes this can be done by an experienced builder without redrawing the plans. If the anticipated changes are too great to handle by merely marking on the existing plans, we suggest you consult a local architect. (Home Planners, Inc., does not make changes in plans.) By presenting him with a set of blueprints to study, you should be saving his time and your money.

6. CAN BLUEPRINTS BE REVERSED? We can reverse the plans for every design in this book; but in doing so, the lettering and dimensions also will appear in reverse. Instead of having plans reversed, some people order standard blueprints and have an experienced contractor build the home in reverse of the standard plans. However, if you are going to make several changes in addition to reversing the plan, it would be well to present the standard blueprints to your local architect for redrawing the plans in reverse—incorporating, at the same time, any changes you prefer. There is no extra charge for reversing our plans.

7. HOW ARE MATERIAL LISTS USED? The material list shows the quantities, types and sizes of materials required to build your home. (Plumbing, heating and electrical materials are excluded because requirements for these are usually decided by the owner in cooperation with local tradespeople.) These lists show where the materials are used, and they provide a column for quickly filling in costs by your material dealer or builder without making a time consuming compilation of the list themselves.

Richard B. Pollman. (See inside back cover.) The following questions and answers have been compiled in anticipation of the many inquiries usually prompted by persons about to purchase blueprints.

8. CAN BLUEPRINTS AND MATERIAL LISTS BE RETURNED? With the exception of reversed plans (see Question 6), blueprints and material lists can be returned for refund or exchange, provided the request is made within ten days, and provided the returned merchandise arrives in salable condition. Care should be taken to return the prints in a mailing tube.

9. HOW MUCH DOES IT COST TO BUILD? Construction costs range up and down from $15 per square foot of liveable floor space depending upon the location, type of home and upon your specifications. If accurate costs are desired, present a set of blueprints and material list to an architect, builder or material dealer, as such an estimate requires detailed computation of a type usually beyond the layman's knowledge—especially in a period of fluctuating prices. Regardless of the outcome, you are assured that all our homes have been planned for the most economical use of building materials, consistent with sound construction and good design.

10. CAN COMPLETED HOMES BE SEEN BEFORE GETTING BLUEPRINTS? Even though nine out of ten of our blueprint buyers expect to build, it is regretted these people do not give us their new locations for the benefit of later customers.

11. WHAT IS THE COST AND DELIVERY TIME OF BLUEPRINTS AND MATERIAL LISTS? Blueprints are $7.50 for one set, or three sets. for $15.00. Material lists are $1.00 each. These are mailed postpaid via parcel post the same day your order and remittance are received. Add 25¢ per order Parcel Post; 50¢ for First Class Mail; $1.00 for Airmail.

ABOUT EASIER F.H.A. TERMS

The recently enacted housing law means lower down payments to homebuyers. The buyer puts down only five percent on the first $9,000, and 25 percent on the balance. He also is entitled to get a mortgage up to $20,000 which can be paid for over 30 years.

The new law means that there are going to be many families who will be able to switch from old houses to new homes; and many families now living in apartments will be tempted to get into a home of their own.

This book was published primarily for such people. It provides a great variety of homes to meet the cultural and physical living requirements of as many different types of families as possible. In order to meet the building budget of most people, the homes presented here fall, for the most part, into the $8,000 to $18,000 price range.

The following table shows what the new law means in terms of down payments, and monthly payments required for new housing.

FHA Appraised Value of House & Lot	Down Payment	Monthly Payment
$ 5,000	$ 250	$ 25.98
7,000	350	36.38
10,000	700	50.87
12,000	1,200	59.08
15,000	1,950	71.38
18,000	2,700	83.69
20,000	3,200	91.90
25,000	5,000	109.40

(Note: Any reader that is eligible for the Veterans Administration Housing provisions will find that agency's down payment requirements even more liberal. The VA office should be contacted for specific information.)

When referring to the above chart, it should be kept in mind that the FHA appraised value for new homes is usually slightly less than the current market price of the house and lot together. This amount should be added to the down payment required.

We sincerely hope that all of our readers will make an effort to investigate further the advantages of these new liberal FHA terms. Expert guidance may be obtained from a local bank, savings and loan association, or mortgage company. The keys to a new home may be yours sooner than you thought possible.

SCALE MODEL DESIGNS

The best way to visualize the home you
are planning is to actually see that home in
miniature. Family Homes Magazine has made
available, through Home Planners, Inc., scale models
for the 16* designs shown on the following
ten pages (26 through 35).
Every kit is in full color to show the exact appearance of
the finished home. One can see the placement
of windows and doors, drives and walks, chimneys
and the garage. Even the landscaping suggestions
are included, with fences, arbors,
shrubbery and trees in actual color.
Included in each kit is a complete set of furniture
to scale which can be cut out and used to study
the furniture arrangements of each room.
A floor plan is included with each model,
and this furniture may be placed on the plan
and located as to windows and wall space.
A scale model, a blueprint, a material list and a specification
outline represent a package of ideas that
will guarantee many enjoyable hours of
home planning adventure and building.

*Note: Scale models are available *only* for the 16 designs in this section.

The arrangement of the plan in this colonial cottage eliminates the use of rooms for halls and creates a feeling of spaciousness in the combined rooms. Generous storage wall closets have been provided and the garage offers ample room for storage and family hobbies.

DESIGN K 1
925 SQ. FT., 10,180 CU. FT.

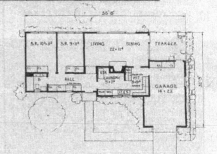

The exterior of this home has been designed with simplicity. The long ledge-rock faced flower box and low roof lines accent the horizontal feeling. A beautiful fireplace, built-in cabinets, book shelves and china-buffet are features of the L-shaped living-dining area.

DESIGN K 3
970 SQ. FT., 10,670 CU. FT.

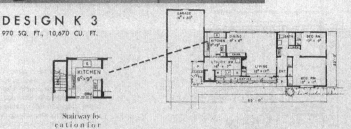

Stairway location for basement.

A small house looks very pretentious when the attached garage is turned sideways. At least 25 feet should be provided for a turning radius, however, on an interior lot. Emphasis has been placed on the living and work center in the plan.

Location of stairway if built with basement. Available blueprints and material lists include optional basement.

DESIGN K 5
1,290 SQ. FT., 14,832 CU. FT.

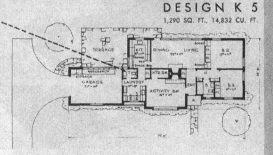

27

DESIGN K 6
1,160 SQ. FT., 12,830 CU. FT.

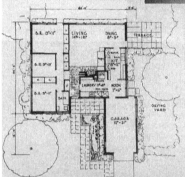

Emphasis has been placed on modern detail combined with a low pitched, overhanging main roof in this design. The exterior walls of colorful ledgerock stone and plywood panels blend into the landscaping and become a natural part of the setting. The large living-dining area has been arranged for functional furniture groupings. Note the convenience of the combined kitchen-nook-laundry. Also, did you see the dramatic pool at the protected front entrance?

DESIGN K 8
14,960 CU. FT.

In this home the friendly feeling of the traditional Cape Cod design has been combined with new convenience features of planning. The bright modern

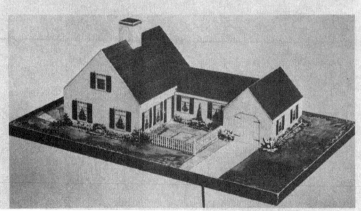

DESIGN K 9

1,300 SQ. FT., 14,224 CU. FT.

This three bedroom home is a modified colonial design of red brick and stained cypress trim. The natural colors of all of the materials blend with the landscaping for a charming effect. The L-shaped plan provides a definite separation of the outdoor living and service yards and has been designed for flexibility of family living.

in-line kitchen, the automatically equipped laundry, radiant heating and storage wall closets are all a part of the new home.

Second Floor Plan 520 SQ. FT.

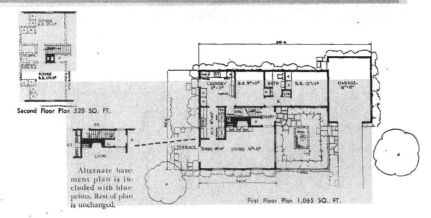

Alternate basement plan is included with blueprints. Rest of plan is unchanged.

First Floor Plan 1,065 SQ. FT.

29

DESIGN K 10
1,170 SQ. FT., 12,872 CU. FT.

The entrance patio of this U-shaped home is characteristic of the
southwest. However, in recent years homes of this type have been spreading

DESIGN K 11
1,024 SQ. FT., 10,180 CU. FT.

Water on the roof? It might surprise
you but the idea is very old, especially in
some commercial and industrial build-
ings. The fact is that it is a fine way to
provide summer comfort economically.
Another feature of this small home is the
rear glass wall facing south and the wide
"sun visor" projection over the glass. Yes,
it is a solar house designed to harness the
low winter sun for heating. The cheerfulness of solar windows adds much joy to
living.

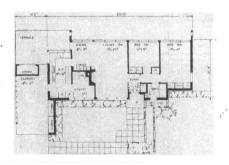

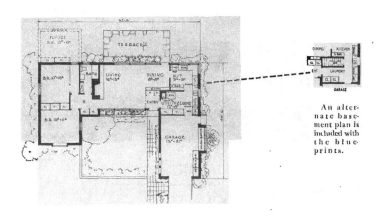

An alternate basement plan is included with the blueprints.

over the entire country and popularly called "Ranch House." Note that arrangements have been made for adding a third bedroom in the plan.

DESIGN K 12

15,784 CU. FT.

In this colonial adaptation, hand split fieldstone and white clapboards are used for a pleasing exterior effect. The lower level activities room is a real center of family living, planned for many uses.

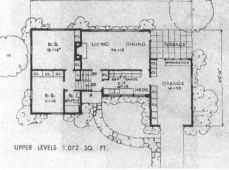

UPPER LEVELS 1,072 SQ. FT.

LOWER LEVEL 542 SQ. FT.

31

DESIGN K 13
1,244 SQ. FT., 16,172 CU. FT.

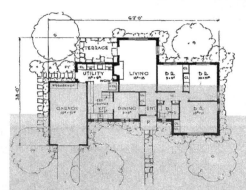

Stained hall timbers and decorative brick patterns are natural materials characteristic of the English cottage designs. Although they are more expensive to use in this way, there is little doubt of their charming effect. The arrangement of the plan affords much privacy for all rooms with cross-room traffic at a minimum.

DESIGN K 15
1,400 SQ. FT., 15,420 CU. FT.

This home has been designed for an active family with varied interests. A large activities room, the den and the living-dining area

DESIGN K 16

13,980 CU. FT.
19,230 CU. FT. (with basement)

This Cape Cod design includes a formal dining room, breakfast nook and a panelled fireplace wall. The radiant heat hot water boiler, water heater and incinerator have been tucked away under the stairway. Did you see the second floor window seats?

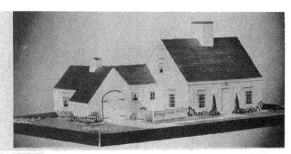

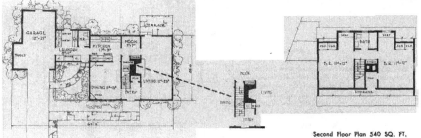

First Floor Plan   900 SQ. FT.

Laundry remains on first floor in alternate basement plan.

Second Floor Plan 540 SQ. FT.

provide the solution to the problem. The den is very useful as a guest room with a washroom so handy off the entrance hall.

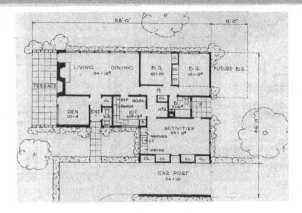

DESIGN K 18
1,086 SQ. FT., 11,962 CU. FT.

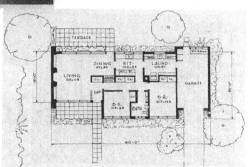

Note how convenient this small home is to live in, the ease of movement from one area to another, the spacious living-dining space with view front and rear. Radiant hot water floor heating with pipe coils buried in the concrete provides a new comfort in living as gentle as the warmth of a spring day. Cold floors and drafts are eliminated, and housekeeping is reduced to a minimum—radiant heating is clean.

DESIGN K 20
1,165 SQ. FT., 12,784 CU. FT.
21,058 CU. FT. (with basement)

A corner lot design should receive some special consideration in planning. Often an L-shaped plan is desirable to provide privacy for the rear garden from the side street. In this home the garage has been used for this screen effect, and at the same time to produce a rambling exterior appearance.

An alternate basement plan is included with the blueprints.

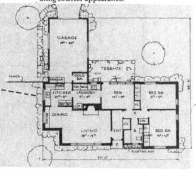

DESIGN K 21
1,043 SQ. FT., 15,122 CU. FT.

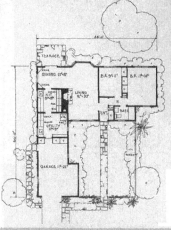

This small Cape Cod cottage has eye appeal.
The L-shaped plan seems to create a rambling
design, and the fence enclosed entrance court with
beautiful flowers and planting offers a pleasant
invitation to step inside. With the garage so near
the street, the winter problem of shoveling snow
is almost negligible. Note the large storage area
and cabinets provided in the garage. The large
living room has an attractive bay window, and
corner cabinets in the dining-L are a pleasant
touch.

DESIGN K 22
1,460 SQ. FT., 18,820 CU. FT.

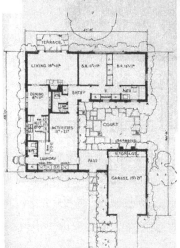

The flagstone paved courtyard of this English cottage is
an unusual feature and affords much privacy in living. There
is a barbecue on the end of the garage for outdoor eating and
plenty of storage space in the garage to put the outdoor
things away in the cold season. Note the interesting arrangement of the kitchen-laundry-activities area. An active family
could really live in this home. A steep stairway near the entrance hall leads to future room or storage space in the attic.

HOMES 1200 TO 1300 SQ. FT.

A subdivision containing all of the homes in this section would soon become the show place of any community. Here are perfect examples of the results to be achieved from ingeniously conceived exteriors and floor plans. Each design is a masterpiece by itself, suitable for the worthy consideration of the most discriminating home owner. Avail yourself at low cost of fine architectural planning. The rewards will be great for years to come.

DESIGN K 75
1,289 SQ. FT., 24,619 CU. FT.

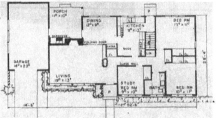

Clean exterior lines catch the eye. The vertical paneling contrasts pleasingly with the wide roof overhang and the quarried stone. The window arrangement helps contribute to the touch of perfection. The floor plan of this design is particularly interesting. There are many unusual features.

DESIGN K 432
1,212 SQ. FT., 12,120 CU. FT.

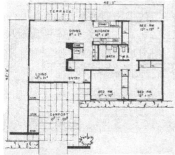

Plumbing costs can often be prohibitive. Here is another Poliman design which shows how good planning can result in lower construction costs. Observe the plumbing of the kitchen, the washroom, the bath and the heater room in relation to one another. Note how the kitchen can be closed off from the dining area by using a folding door.

DESIGN K 220
1,228 SQ. FT., 12,503 CU. FT.

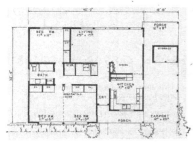

Dual use space is not only most practical and convenient, but also the most desirable way to get the most for your building dollar. A large living-dining area promotes conversational groupings and provides plenty of recreational space during holiday get-togethers. Furniture placement becomes more flexible. The two bedrooms, when opened up, provide an all-purpose area on rainy days.

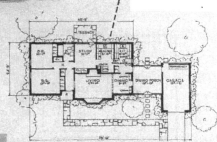

DESIGN K 17

**1,235 SQ. FT., 13,630 CU. FT.
19,764 CU. FT. (with basement)**

This small home of hand split fieldstone masquerades as a large home most successfully. The incorporation of the porch and garage into the residential design gives commanding breadth to the whole structure. The large picture window bay in the spacious living-dining area adds a pleasant note. The study again appears as a dual use space so necessary to family needs and is used as an outlet to the rear garden.

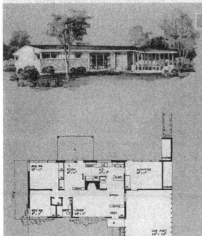

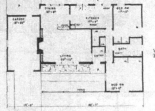

DESIGN K 277

1,248 SQ. FT., 12,336 CU. FT.

The unusual layout of this plan demands study to be fully appreciated. Note its openness — how the vestibule, living, dining, kitchen-laundry and study form one big area; yet they are distinctly set apart by the china, snack bar (with cabinets above), draw drape and bookshelves.

DESIGN K 89

1,232 SQ. FT., 22,714 CU. FT.

Note the excellent traffic circulation, the dining-L separated by a china with planting on top, the charm of bookshelves on each side of the fireplace, the double wardrobe closets in each bedroom, the nook, and the large vanity. Don't overlook the porch off the dining area.

DESIGN K 29
1,281 SQ. FT., 12,993 CU. FT.

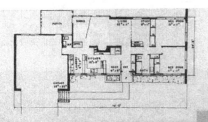

Notice how the study or third bedroom can be made a part of the living-dining area by sliding back the folding wall. In addition to good traffic circulation and a conveniently located porch, you will find plenty of closets, cabinets and built-ins.

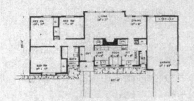

DESIGN K 30
1,266 SQ. FT., 14,110 CU. FT.

Simplicity lends distinction to this clean-cut three bedroom home planned for efficient living. Notice the pleasing contrast of vertical V-groove boards and the long horizontal line of the window shading roof overhang, which joins the flat roofed garage.

DESIGN K 283
1,232 SQ. FT., 12,381 CU. FT.

A clear-through living-dining area with adjoining terrace, a large nook area in the kitchen with built-in china, well lighted and cheerful laundry, a spacious master bedroom, generous closets and large carport storage areas all work to make this a most desirable design.

DESIGN K 383
1,300 SQ. FT., 12,232 CU. FT.

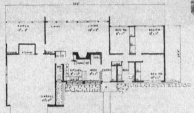

Enjoy the outdoors! Brightness and beauty are given by the large windows which comprise the entire outside wall of the living-dining area. The functional island with fireplace unifies this area with the practical kitchen-nook. No traffic jams here.

DESIGN K 278
1,230 SQ. FT., 20,917 CU. FT.

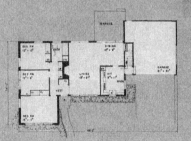

This type of plan has proven itself very popular. The cheerfulness of the living area is enhanced by the fireplace and the floor-to-ceiling panel windows on both ends. The dining-L off the kitchen makes the living area appear spacious. The built-in china and the dining terrace are practical features, too.

DESIGN K 301
1,237 SQ. FT., 24,440 CU. FT.

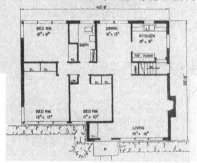

Completely poised with the knowledge of its own competence, this little house stands four-square upon its plot and yields ground to no other. A study of the floor plan will disclose three bedrooms and bath. Many closets. The living room-dining room-kitchen section is conservative in treatment.

DESIGN K 371
1,236 SQ. FT., 21,380 CU. FT.

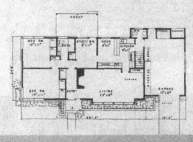

For convenient living, the various activities of the daily routine must be well provided for. There is plenty of storage space both inside and out. The bath and washroom are extremely well situated. Areas for formal and informal dining are provided. Stairs to basement located for utmost utility. The covered porch enhances summer enjoyment.

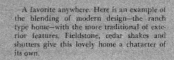

DESIGN K 186
1,229 SQ. FT., 15,100 CU. FT.

Stairway location if built with basement.

A favorite anywhere. Here is an example of the blending of modern design—the ranch type home—with the more traditional of exterior features. Fieldstone, cedar shakes and shutters give this lovely home a character of its own.

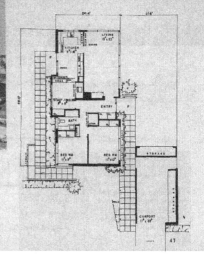

DESIGN K 384
1,239 SQ. FT., 11,947 CU. FT.

The privacy fence allows for the best possible use of large areas of glass on the suburban site. Windows on two sides of the living area make the outdoors and inside seem as one. The two open sides of the fireplace stimulate both the appearance and the feeling of warmth.

1½ STORY HOMES

A 1½ story home containing 1300 square feet can be constructed more economically than a one story ranch home having the same amount of square footage. This means that the story-and-a-half home represents the greater return on your building dollar. The homes on the following pages represent additional economy since the young family need not finish off the second floor until the budget permits or until the size of the family necessitates. The homes in this section may be the answer to your housing problem.

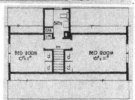

DESIGN K 178
20,097 CU. FT.

First Floor Plan   957 SQ. FT.

Here is a story-and-a-half design preserving the best of the old features and incorporating the most outstanding of the new. Note the two baths, the windowed expanse of the dining room, and the extensive closet space.

Second Floor Plan 488 SQ. FT.

DESIGN K 194
12,628 CU. FT.

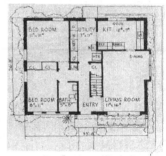

First Floor Plan   902 SQ. FT.

Build in the present and prepare for the future. This story and a half home will more than adequately service the growing family. The second floor gives you two large bedrooms and plenty of storage space. Provisions are made for a second bath.

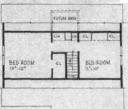

Second Floor Plan 437 SQ. FT.

DESIGN K 182
13,622 CU. FT.

Here is your story-and-a-half home with economy of space. High silled windows free you from the vexing problem of finding wall space for your furniture. The roomy second floor provides three closets, a big storage area, a washroom and a built-in vanity.

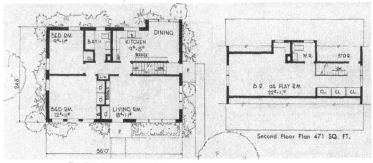

First Floor Plan   906 SQ. FT.

Second Floor Plan 471 SQ. FT.

DESIGN K 144
16,744 CU. FT.

Four bedrooms, two baths, a separate dining area and a vestibule! This is truly a budget home with big home features. Observe the two china cabinets to each side of the arch leading into the dinette. A growing family could finish the second floor as needed.

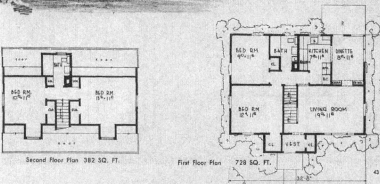

Second Floor Plan 382 SQ. FT.

First Floor Plan   728 SQ. FT.

DESIGN K 28
20,844 CU. FT.

There's no need to cramp when seven rooms and two baths can be designed into 1412 square feet of livable floor area, in addition to the basement. The combination of wide wood siding (or cedar shakes), vertical boards and battens, and fieldstone provide a long lasting charm to the exterior.

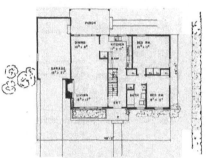

First Floor Plan 956 SQ. FT.

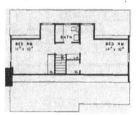

Second Floor Plan 456 SQ. FT.

The building dollar stretches the farthest when it is used on a 1½ or 2 story home. Here is proof that a four bedroom home does not have to be an expensive one. Its attractive exterior lines are characteristic of Richard B. Pollman's designs. Note the planting area in front of the large living room windows.

DESIGN K 254
16,702 CU. FT.

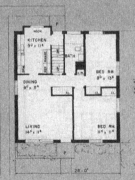

First Floor Plan 813 SQ. FT.

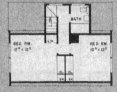

Second Floor Plan 464 SQ. FT.

44

DESIGN K 114
23,882 CU. FT.

Four bedrooms and two baths come as something of a surprise in a house that appears so small. The attractive first floor encompasses a great deal of living space, too. Don't overlook the two built-in chests in both second floor bedrooms. The available blueprints of plans by Architects Palmquist & Wright include detailed drawings of the second floor.

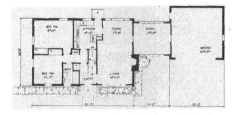

First Floor Plan   1,080 SQ. FT.

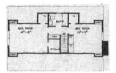

Second Floor Plan 598 SQ. FT.

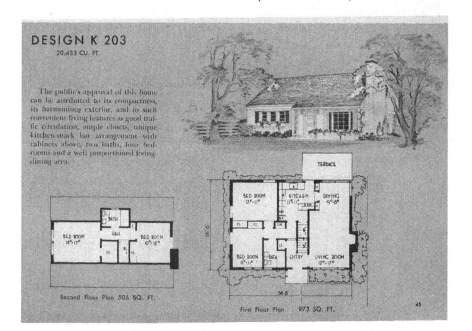

DESIGN K 203
20,433 CU. FT.

The public's approval of this home can be attributed to its compactness, its harmonious exterior, and to such convenient living features as good traffic circulation, ample closets, unique kitchen-snack bar arrangement with cabinets above, two baths, four bedrooms and a well proportioned living-dining area.

Second Floor Plan 506 SQ. FT.

First Floor Plan   973 SQ. FT.

45

DESIGN K 287
22,637 CU. FT.

Here's a home that will grow old gracefully. It will provide a family with a place for everything, and with everything in its place. Notice the excellent traffic circulation, the private terrace and the unusual vestibule. Study the plan and see how many features you can find.

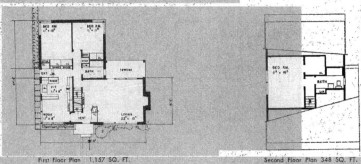

First Floor Plan   1,157 SQ. FT.

Second Floor Plan 348 SQ. FT.

DESIGN K 374
21,416 CU. FT.

Warmth and true "homey" charm are reflected in this beautiful 1½ story four bedroom home. Lots of windows, a bath on each floor, centralized stairways, ample closet space and the roomy kitchen with snack bar assure family living at its best. A full size basement increases its living possibilities.

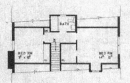

Second Floor Plan 466 SQ. FT.

First Floor Plan   975 SQ. FT.

DESIGN K 361
20,307 CU. FT.

The roof overhang of the 1½ story home can be just as attractive as that of the ranch home. Here's proof. The planting box between the living and dining areas provides added interest. Plans and specifications are prepared by Architects Palmquist & Wright.

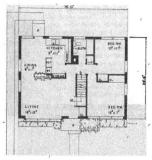

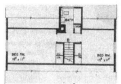

Second Floor Plan 488 SQ. FT.

First Floor Plan 967 SQ. FT.

DESIGN K 233
21,138 CU. FT.

A story-and-a-half home with Early American Farmhouse styling. The fieldstone fireplace (complete with raised flagstone hearth, woodbox and with shelves above) adds to its charm.

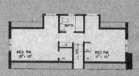

Second Floor Plan 448 SQ. FT.

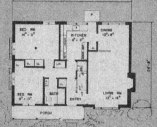

First Floor Plan 1,002 SQ. FT.

47

SAVE—TIME and MONEY

BLUEPRINTS

There is a blueprint for every home shown in this book. These ready-to-build, professional plans were prepared by the firm of Palmquist & Wright, members of the American Institute of Architects. All necessary dimensions, views, details and elevations are included. In addition to using them for building, blueprints became indispensable as a further aid to your home planning study and for determining building costs.

1 Set $7.50; 2 Sets $12.50; 3 Sets $15.00; For every Set over 3, add $5.00

MATERIAL LISTS

Material lists also are available for every design. Each list shows you the quantity, type and size of the materials required to build your home. They also tell you where these materials are used. This makes them easy to understand. Material lists simplify your material ordering and enable you to get quicker price quotations from your builder and material dealer. Be sure to request material lists with your blueprints.

Material Lists are only $1.00 each

SPECIFICATION OUTLINES

With each blueprint order, you receive a twelve page specification outline at no additional cost. This fill-in type specification lists 150 phases of home construction—from excavating to painting. Use it for specifying to your builder the exact equipment and methods of construction you want in your next home.

IMPORTANT BEFORE YOU ORDER BLUEPRINTS

(We suggest you review the points listed below, which usually are brought up by prospective plan buyers.)

• The square and cubic footages shown for each design do not include garages, carports, breezeways or porches.

• Contractors' prices range up and down from about $15 per square foot, depending upon location, specifications and type of home. They must have a set of blueprints and material list to give you an exact price for building.

• Three to six sets of blueprints are required for building: one each for builder, owner, permit, F. H. A. or V. A., mortgage banker and tradesmen.

• All plans are drawn to meet or exceed F. H. A., V. A. and local code requirements.

• Home Planners, Inc., the source for these plans, does not make changes in blueprints. Present blueprints to local architect, builder or material dealer for changes. They will mark minor changes on existing plans or redraw them for major changes.

• Houses can be reversed on blueprints. Kindly write directly to Home Planners before ordering such reverse plans.

HOW AND WHERE TO ORDER: Blueprints, material lists, and books may be ordered directly from Home Planners, Inc., 16310 Grand River, Detroit 27, Michigan. Your remittance may be in the form of a check or money order. Shipments may be made on a C. O. D. basis. Please indicate method of shipment (prepaid or C. O. D.) and add 25¢ for Parcel Post, 50¢ for First Class, or $1.00 for Air Mail Service.

FOUR MORE BOOKS OF DESIGNS—ALL FOR 2.00!

by RICHARD B. POLLMAN

200 HOMES—
ALL SIZES AND TYPES

Here are 96 pages containing 200 different exteriors and floor plans. This book is a selected collection of proven popular designs. It is one you should not be without. when planning your next home. This outstanding collection is sectionalized according to size. You'll profit from the many ideas found in this book. Exceptional value! Price $1.00

66 CONTEMPORARY HOMES

The latest trend in today's design is illustrated in this outstanding book of 48 pages containing 66 designs for family living. You'll see practical applications of such truly up-to-the-minute features as privacy fences, carports, glass walls, inside baths, open planning, and dual use space. Be sure your next home is designed for Convenient Living. Price 50¢

HOMES OF NATURAL STONE

The increasing popularity of quarried stone makes this book very timely. It contains 32 delightful homes of all types; 1, 1½, and 2 story; small, medium, large; with and without basement; contemporary and traditional; some with a little stone and some with a lot. Also shown are 15 pages of outdoor and indoor fireplaces, planters, patio settings, garden walks, interesting fences, and activities rooms. Worth more than this modest price! Price 50¢

FAMILY HOMES

This interesting book contains 50 plans for building . . . plans especially suited for real family living. It includes a wide variety of home types and shows 90 absorbing illustrations of exteriors and interiors. You'll see such up-to-the-minute features as folding walls and doors, dual use space, open planning, organized storage and built-ins. Jammed with value! Price 50¢

CLIP and MAIL

for

FAST SERVICE

PLEASE SEND ME THE FOLLOWING

_____Blueprints for Designs #_____ #_____ #_____ #_____ $ _____
(1 Set $7.50; 2 Sets $12.50; 3 Sets $15.00; For every set over 3, add $5.00)

_____Material lists @ $1.00 each for Designs #_____ #_____ ...... $ _____

_____¼" Scale Models @ $2.00 each, available only for the following Designs:... $ _____
E1, 3, 5, 6, 8, 9, 10, 11, 12, 13, 15, 16, 18, 20, 21 & 22*
Circle Design #'s wanted. No other Scale Models are available.

_____"Family Homes" books @ 50¢ each.................................. $ _____

_____"Homes of Natural Stone" books @ 50¢ each.......................... $ _____

_____"200 Homes" books @ $1.00 each................................... $ _____

_____"66 Contemporary Homes" books @ 50¢ each......................... $ _____

_____All Four Books Above For $2.00.................................... $ _____

_____"100 Homes" books @ $1.00 (See inside front cover)................. $ _____

Michigan residents add 3% Sales Tax $ _____

Check ▶ ☐ Parcel Post   ☐ First Class   ☐ Air Mail   ☐ C.O.D.-Pay   (C.O.D. & Parcel Post)
✓ One   Add 25¢   Add 50¢   Add $1.00   Postman   (limited to U.S.A. only)

PLEASE PRINT   TOTAL { $ _____
                                              { $ _____

NAME_____ADDRESS_____

CITY_____ZONE_____STATE_____

SAVE–TIME and MONEY

BLUEPRINTS

There is a blueprint for every home shown in this book. These ready-to-build professional plans were prepared by the firm of Palmquist & Wright, members of the American Institute of Architects. All necessary dimensions, views, details and elevations are included. In addition to using them for building, blueprints become indispensable as a further aid to your home planning study and for determining building costs.

1 Set $7.50; 2 Sets $12.50; 3 Sets $15.00; For every Set over 3, add $5.00

MATERIAL LISTS

Material lists also are available for every design. Each list shows you the quantity, type and size of the materials required to build your home. They also tell you where these materials are used. This makes them easy to understand. Material lists simplify your material ordering and enable you to get quicker price quotations from your builder and material dealer. Be sure to request material lists with your blueprints.

Material Lists are only $1.00 each

SPECIFICATION OUTLINES

With each blueprint order, you receive a twelve page specification outline at no additional cost. This fill-in type specification lists 150 phases of home construction—from excavating to painting. Use it for specifying to your builder the exact equipment and methods of construction you want in your next home.

············ CLIP and MAIL

for

FAST SERVICE

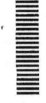

CPSIA information can be obtained
at www.ICGtesting.com
Printed in the USA
BVHW041122131221
623919BV00007B/328